THE BEST BOOK OF

Endangered and Extinct Animals

Christiane Gunzi

KINGFISHER

BOSTON

Contents

KINGFISHER

a Houghton Mifflin Company imprint
222 Berkeley Street
Boston, Massachusetts 02116
www.houghtonmifflinbooks.com

Created for Kingfisher Publications Plc
by Picthall & Gunzi Limited

Author and editor: Christiane Gunzi
Designer: Dominic Zwemmer
Consultant: Barbara Taylor-Cork

Illustrators: Michael Langham-Rowe,
Angus McBride, Richard Hook, Peter
Goodfellow, Ray Grinaway, Bernard
Long, Tony Morris, Nicki Palin

First published by Kingfisher
Publications Plc 2004

10 9 8 7 6 5 4 3 2 1

1TR/0304/WKT/MAR(MAR)/128KMA

Copyright © Kingfisher
Publications Plc 2004

LIBRARY OF CONGRESS CATALOGING-IN-PUBLICATION DATA
has been applied for

ISBN 0-7534-5757-1

Printed in China.

4 What is extinction?

6 Extinct animals of the world

14 The end of the Ice Age

16 Where did the dodo go?

24 The great survivors

26 Extinction and us

8 How we know

10 When the dinosaurs died

12 Amazing reptiles

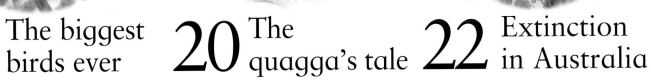

18 The biggest birds ever

20 The quagga's tale

22 Extinction in Australia

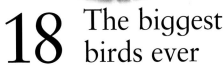

28 Wildlife at risk

30 A future for all of us

31 Glossary

32 Index

What is extinction?

Extinction is the end of a species—a group of animals or plants. Extinct animals are those that no longer exist such as dinosaurs and woolly mammoths. Before humans existed extinctions were caused by natural events and took many years. But since humans arrived many animal species have died out in a very short space of time.

A change of climate
Many animals, such as woolly mammoths, died out at the end of the last Ice Age, when the climate became warmer.

Destroying habitats
People are damaging the habitats where wild animals live. Huge areas of forests have been cut down to make room for farms and buildings. This is the most common cause of extinction today.

Fishing too much
At the moment we are catching too many fish in the oceans. This is known as "overharvesting." If we do not stop overfishing very soon, many species of fish will become extinct.

Introducing species
When people first traveled to other countries, they took dogs, cats, and pigs with them. These animals competed with the animals that already lived there and ate their eggs and young.

Mass extinctions

Major extinctions are known
as mass extinctions. In a mass
extinction many species die out
at the same time. There have been
at least five big mass extinctions.
Many scientists believe that the
last one was caused when an
enormous meteor crashed into
Earth. It would have caused
dramatic changes in climate,
including floods.

A huge meteor probably
brought about the end of
dinosaurs and pterosaurs.

Extinct animals of the world

During billions of years of life on Earth millions of species of animals have evolved and then died out. The most well-known extinct animals are the dinosaurs, which died out 65 million years ago. But many animals have become extinct since then, and others will continue to die out in the future. The Tasmanian tiger, or thylacine, only became extinct 100 years ago.

Pteranodon died out 65 million years ago.

Archelon died out 65 million years ago.

Argentinosaurus died out 65 million years ago.

Dunkleosteus (left) died out 360 million years ago.

The early extinctions

The mass extinction of dinosaurs and other animals was a huge event, but there were at least four other mass extinctions before that one. *Dunkleosteus* and many other sea creatures became extinct 360 million years ago in the Devonian period.

Mosasaurs died out 65 million years ago.

Ammonites died out 65 million years ago.

Platybelodon
died out 1.75 million years ago.

Steller's sea cow
died out in 1768.

Giant moa died
out at the end
of the 1600s.

Macrauchenias
died out 20,000
years ago.

Dodo died out
in 1681.

Quagga died out
in 1870.

Smilodon
died out 10,000 years ago.

Carolina parakeet
died out in 1920.

Woolly rhinoceros died
out 10,000 years ago.

Thylacine (Tasmanian tiger)
died out in the 1930s.

How we know

Scientists learn about extinct animals by studying fossils.
The fossilized bones of dinosaurs show us what these amazing reptiles looked like and how they lived millions of years ago. The fossilized shells that you find on beaches belong to sea creatures that swam in the oceans before even the dinosaurs existed!

Oceans of animals

Around 600 million years ago a huge variety of wildlife lived in the oceans, and sea creatures with shells started to appear. But these animals died out in a series of mass extinctions, possibly owing to changes in sea levels. Their fossils still remain today.

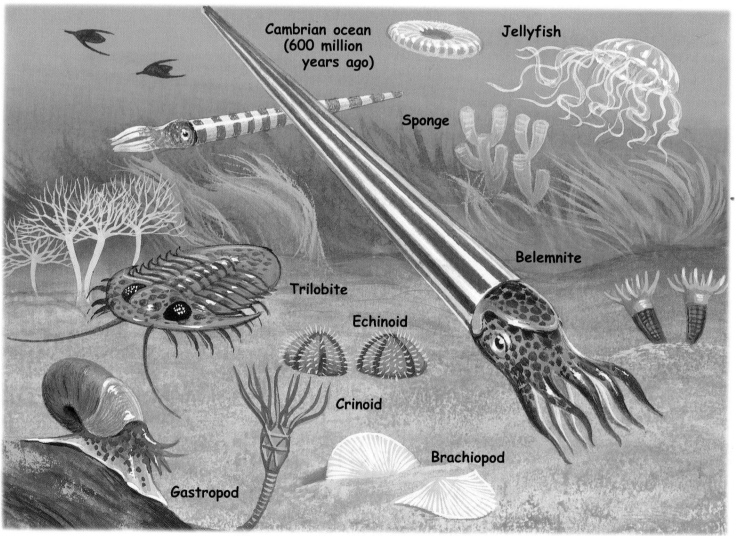

Cambrian ocean (600 million years ago)

Jellyfish

Sponge

Belemnite

Trilobite

Echinoid

Crinoid

Brachiopod

Gastropod

How an ammonite fossil is formed

1 When a shelled sea creature dies, its shell falls onto the seabed. The animal's soft body dissolves, but the shell remains.

2 As the sea gently washes over the shell, sand and sediment gradually fill up inside. Eventually the shell is completely covered.

3 Over millions of years the sand and sediment harden into rock in the shape of the shelled creature. A fossil has formed.

4 After many more years a fossil hunter can break open a rock to discover the fossil of an extinct ammonite hidden inside.

Finding fossils

Studying fossils helps us understand more about animals. There are fossils of ammonites on many beaches all over the world. It is very exciting to look at the remains of an animal that lived in the ocean 200 million years ago!

These children are looking at an ammonite fossil with their teacher.

When the dinosaurs died

For 165 million years dinosaurs ruled Earth. Then 65 million years ago, at the end of the Cretaceous period, they all died out. This is the most famous mass extinction, even though it was not as big as some of the earlier ones. When the dinosaurs became extinct, many other animals did too. Amazingly, some survived, including insects, lizards, crocodiles, a few mammals, birds, and many fish and other sea creatures.

Dinosaurs could not survive when huge dust clouds blocked out the warm sun for many years.

Dangerous dust cloud

The end of the dinosaurs was probably caused by the climate becoming cooler. At that time there were huge volcanoes pumping ash into the sky, and a huge meteor crashed into Earth. Ash and dust made the planet dark and cold for many years.

11

Amazing reptiles

Many amazing reptiles died out when the dinosaurs did. These included enormous flying reptiles and huge, powerful sea reptiles. Some swimming reptiles, such as *Liopleurodon*, were as long as the biggest long-necked dinosaurs. By the end of the Cretaceous period pterosaurs, mosasaurs, and plesiosaurs were all extinct. From this time onward mammals began to rule Earth.

Mega crocodile

The largest crocodile that ever lived was *Deinosuchus*. It was 49 ft. (15m) long and might have weighed two tons. This huge reptile ate dinosaurs!

Reptiles of the sea

Sea reptiles, such as *Platecarpus* and *Liopleurodon*, were fierce predators. Some sea reptiles grew to gigantic sizes and were as big as sperm whales are today. Their teeth were twice the size of *T. rex*'s teeth!

Platecarpus was a mosasaur around 23 ft. (7m) long.

Elasmosaurus' neck was more than half the length of its body.

Ammonites swam using jet propulsion.

Reptiles of the sky

The biggest flying creatures ever were reptiles called pterosaurs. Pterosaurs had wings like a bat's, and their bodies were probably furry.

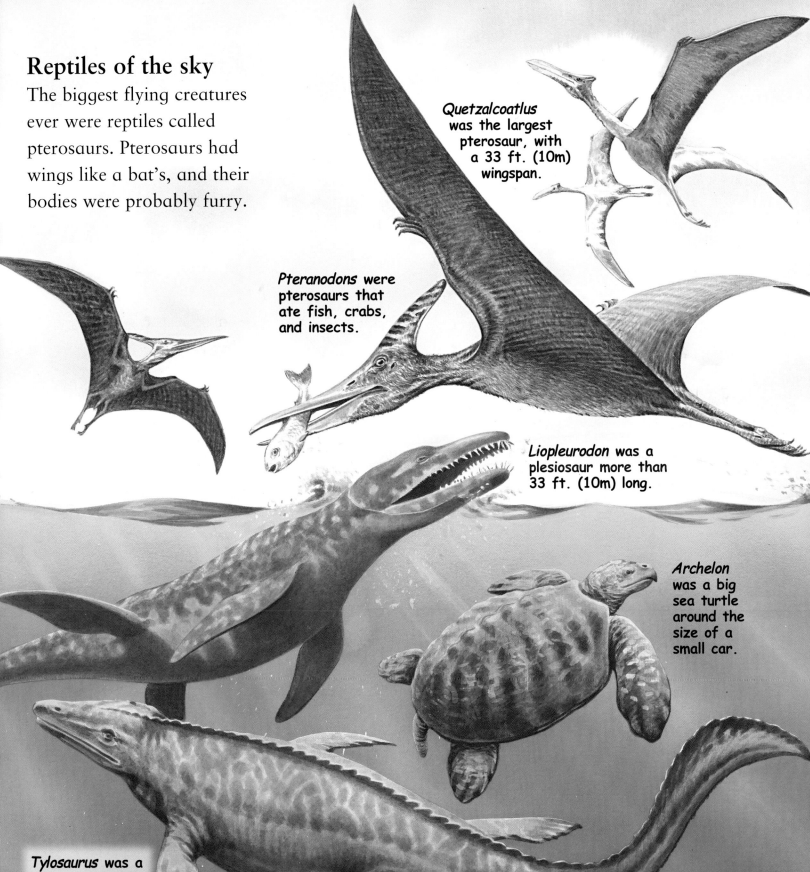

Quetzalcoatlus was the largest pterosaur, with a 33 ft. (10m) wingspan.

Pteranodons were pterosaurs that ate fish, crabs, and insects.

Liopleurodon was a plesiosaur more than 33 ft. (10m) long.

Archelon was a big sea turtle around the size of a small car.

Tylosaurus was a large, carnivorous mosasaur up to 39 ft. (12m) long.

Woolly rhinoceroses grazed on grasslands and tundra.

Woolly mammoths fiercely protected their young from attackers such as lions.

Mighty mammoths

With their long, hairy coats, woolly mammoths were very well adapted to life in the last Ice Age. In the summer they probably molted, like musk oxen. Most woolly mammoths were the size of today's elephants, but they had huge tusks to defend themselves against enemies.

Cave bears lived in caves close to forests and were the size of the biggest grizzly bears today.

Cave lions hunted plant eaters, such as deer, and became extinct when their prey did.

The end of the Ice Age

Around 10,000 years ago, at the end of the last Ice Age, **many mammals died out.** Summer and winter temperatures became so extreme that big plant eaters, such as woolly mammoths, woolly rhinoceroses, and cave bears, could not adapt to the changes in climate. They were also hunted by humans for their meat and fur, and by the end of the Ice Age they were extinct.

Discovering the past

In 1977 a bulldozer driver in Siberia discovered the frozen carcass of an entire baby mammoth. It was the same size as a baby elephant, but its ears were smaller. Using special radiocarbon dating, scientists discovered that the mammoth had died 40,000 years ago. It still had some hair on its legs!

Where did the dodo go?

The dodo is probably the best-known extinct animal of all. This large, heavy bird was discovered on the island of Mauritius in the Indian Ocean in the 1500s. But, 170 years later, there were no dodos left. Dodos had no real enemies on their island home until European sailors arrived, so they were not afraid of people. Dodos could not fly, and they moved so slowly that they were easy to catch. The sailors mostly killed them for food.

Introducing new species

When sailors traveled to other islands, they took domestic animals with them. They introduced dogs, cats, pigs, and also rats to islands where these animals had never lived before. These "introduced species" competed with the native animals for their food and territory.

Portuguese sailors traveled to the island of Mauritius, taking domestic animals with them.

Disturbed by dogs

The dogs, pigs, and other animals that the sailors brought to the island of Mauritius disturbed the dodos on their nests. These animals may also have eaten the birds' eggs.

All that a dodo had for protection against attackers was its big, strong beak.

The biggest birds ever

Around 400 hundred years ago there were giant moas in New Zealand and elephant birds in Madagascar. These birds could not fly and were probably related to ostriches. Moas did not even have wings! Some moas were the size of a turkey, but others were almost 7 ft. (2m) tall. They lived in forests and fed on plants. People hunted giant moas until they were extinct by the end of the 1600s. Elephant birds died out at arouond the same time.

Enormous eggs

Elephant birds were around 10 ft. (3m) tall, and their eggs were the size of basketballs! These African birds may have died out because people kept stealing their huge eggs for food.

Egg   Basketball

Terrifying talons

A moa's only enemy, aside from humans, was the huge Haast's eagle. This was the largest, most powerful eagle ever known. The Haast's eagle had talons as big as a tiger's claws, and it could swoop down at 50mph (80km/h) to grab a moa. Haast's eagles died out when their moa prey became extinct.

Haast's eagles attacked giant moas in their forest habitat.

The quagga's tale

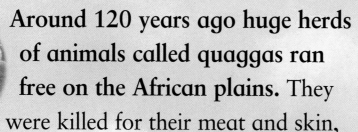

Around 120 years ago huge herds of animals called quaggas ran free on the African plains. They were killed for their meat and skin, and now they do not exist. Recently scientists have discovered that the quagga was actually a type of zebra. Today scientists are trying to breed zebras with markings similar to the quagga. Maybe quaggas will return to Africa someday.

The last quagga

Wild quaggas died out in around 1878. In 1883 the last quagga died at Amsterdam zoo in the Netherlands. She had lived there for 16 years.

Hunting the whole herd

In the 1830s Dutch farmers called Boers, who lived in southern Africa, hunted herds of quagga on horseback. They shot many thousands of them with guns, mostly for food.

Quaggas looked like zebras, but they had fewer stripes.

A strange sight

During the 1830s quaggas were transported to Europe from Africa. These unusual animals were so easy to tame that they were used to pull carriages. Nobody realized then that less than 50 years later quaggas would be extinct.

Extinction in Australia

There are many fascinating animals in Australia, but there used to be even more. Once there were 20 different types of giant kangaroos—as well as wolves and lions with pouches! In the past 200 years one half of all the native mammals of Australia have become extinct. This is mostly owing to hunting and habitat destruction. Other large animals, such as giant lizards, have also died out.

Kangaroo carnivores

One extinct kangaroo was a meat eater. Ekaltadeta was the size of a large dog. It had long teeth used for biting its prey, and it probably used its front legs to hold its food!

Biggest ever

Mammals with pouches, called marsupials, first appeared in the middle of the Cretaceous period. Procoptodon was the biggest kangaroo, and the marsupial lion was the largest carnivorous Australian mammal. Diprotodon was the biggest marsupial ever! All of these marsupials are now extinct. Giant reptiles are extinct, too.

Procoptodon was 10 ft. (3m) tall, with long arms.

Diprotodon was around the size of a cow.

The marsupial lion was 5 ft. (1.5m) from head to tail.

Giant echidna was 3 ft. (1m) long.

Quinkana was a 23 ft. (7m) crocodile with long legs.

The giant ripper lizard was called "megalania."

The tiger with a pouch

The thylacine, or Tasmanian tiger, once lived all over Australia and Tasmania. But when European settlers arrived, they began to kill them. Thylacines ate birds, kangaroos, and small rodents. They also preyed on sheep, so farmers often shot, trapped, and poisoned them. The last known thylacine died in a zoo in 1936.

Thylacines could open their mouths extremely wide in order to bite large animals.

The great survivors

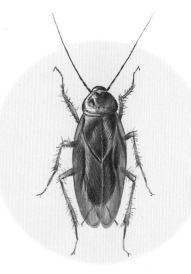

Scientists are not sure why some species survive better than others. Some animals, such as sharks, crocodiles, and insects, are so well adapted to their environments that they have survived unchanged for millions of years. The best survivors are usually animals that can move fast, breed quickly, and eat a variety of foods. Insects do all of these things, and they are able to live in a wide range of places because they are so small. This makes them great survivors.

Incredible insect
Cockroaches have existed for 300 million years, and there are around 4,000 types. These insects can survive for three months without food and one month without water.

Amazing reptile
There have been crocodiles on Earth for 200 million years, and they have hardly changed at all since the time of the dinosaurs. Crocodiles have the most advanced brains of all of the reptiles. They have an extra eyelid to protect their eyes, and they can close their nostrils, ears, and throat in order to dive underwater.

King of the ocean

Sharks are fish that live in every ocean of the world. They have survived for more than 350 million years. One of the earliest types of sharks was around 30 ft. (12m) long. Each one of its huge teeth was around the size of a child's hand!

Not extinct yet

In 1938 an extraordinary fish called a coelacanth was found living in the Indian Ocean. Until then scientists had believed that this type of fish had been extinct for around 70 million years. This ancient fish has been nicknamed a "living fossil."

With its armor plating, powerful tail, and sharp teeth, the Nile crocodile is a perfect predator.

Extinction and us

According to many scientists, a sixth mass extinction is happening right now. They think that humans are the cause. As we pollute the rivers and seas with toxic chemicals and cut down and burn the forests, we are destroying the homes of several species. Animals are dying out at an incredible rate, including unusual insects and sea creatures. It could take millions of years for these animal species to be replaced by new ones.

A fragile world

When people swim over reefs and touch the corals, they damage this delicate habitat and can kill the corals. Reefs that are close to the coast are also damaged by mining, getting buried under layers of mud.

The anchors of boats cause a lot of damage to corals on a reef.

Overfishing in the oceans

One of the most serious problems for the environment today is overharvesting of the oceans. Fish are being caught and killed much faster than they can lay eggs. The fancy seafood known as caviar is actually fish eggs that come from the sturgeon. Surprisingly, some of the most endangered fish of all (see pictures below) are cod and tuna.

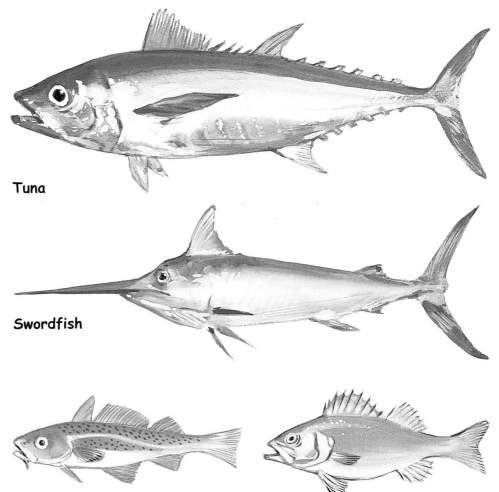

Tuna

Swordfish

Cod

Sea bass

Sturgeon

Monkfish

Spider
monkey

The riches of the rain forest

The Amazon rain forest in South America is the richest wildlife habitat on Earth. It is the home of billions of creatures. All of them are in danger of extinction because so much of the rain forest has been damaged by people.

Macaws

Harpy eagle

Boa
constrictor

Toucan

Jaguar

Capuchin monkey

Amazon
parrot

Hummingbird

Poison
dart
frog

Blue morpho
butterfly

Katydid

Wildlife at risk

The forests are the world's most important habitats. Rain forests, in particular, are home to a huge variety of insects, birds, mammals, reptiles, and amphibians. So far zoologists have been able to identify and name only a small number of the billions of different creatures on Earth. But there are still millions more to discover—especially insects and other tiny creatures. Sadly, some of these animals may become extinct before we even have time to identify them.

Orangutans in danger

All the great apes, such as orangutans and gorillas, are in danger owing to the destruction of the rain forests. In ten to 20 years orangutans will probably be extinct in the wild.

People and trees

In Asia and South America some local people earn a living by cutting down trees. They sell the wood to other, richer countries for making furniture. Wildlife organizations are trying to stop this trade in exotic wood because these trees are very rare, and the rain forests are disappearing.

These trees will be made into furniture.

A future for all of us

Humans are the most powerful and successful species on Earth. We will probably survive for a long time. In order to make sure that tigers, whales, and other endangered animals survive too, we have to take more care of their habitats such as rain forests, oceans, and polar regions. If we do not act in a responsible way, some of the most magnificent animals that have ever lived may become extinct during our lifetimes.

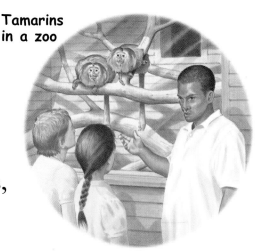

Tamarins in a zoo

Saving the tamarins

Golden lion tamarins live in zoos because their rain forest home in Brazil has been cut down. They are kept behind glass in order to protect them from human diseases. Some of these monkeys have now been returned to the wild.

Too late for the tiger?

There are now only a few thousand wild tigers left. Wildlife organizations are trying to protect these cats, but sadly it could be too late.

Bengal tigers are in danger because of people mining in their territory.

Glossary

adapt To be able to change to fit in with new surroundings. Some animals and plants are good at adapting to change.

amphibian Certain animals, such as frogs and toads, that first appeared on Earth during the Devonian period.

camouflage The different colors and markings on an animal that help it hide in the wild.

carcass The dead body of an animal, often one that is killed for food.

carnivore An animal, such as a shark, hawk, or tiger, that eats meat.

climate The conditions of an area such as its weather and temperature.

Cretaceous period A time period in Earth's history that lasted 65 million years, in which flowering plants first appeared.

Devonian period A time period that lasted 50 million years, in which amphibians first appeared.

domestic animal An animal, such as a dog, that lives with, or is kept by, people.

endangered Animals, such as the Bengal tiger, that are now in danger of becoming extinct.

evolve To develop over time. It can take millions of years for a new species to evolve.

extinct An animal or plant that has died out forever.

fossil The remains of a plant or an animal that died millions of years ago, preserved in rock.

habitat An animal's habitat is its natural home.

ice age A period during which most of Earth's surface was covered in ice.

introduced species Animals that have been taken to a country where they did not live before.

mammals Animals, such as bears, that have fur or hair, give birth to live young, and feed them milk.

meteor A rocklike object from outer space that enters Earth's atmosphere.

native Animals or plants that live in a specific place. The dodo was native to Mauritius.

predators Animals that hunt and prey on other animals.

prey Animals that are hunted and eaten by carnivores.

radiocarbon dating A scientific test carried out on rocks, fossils, and trees to figure out their age.

reptiles Certain cold-blooded animals with scaly skin such as lizards.

species A group of animals that look alike and are closely related to each other.

territory An area of land where an animal lives and that it defends against other animals.

Index

A

Amazon rain forest 28, 29
ammonites 6, 9, 12
Archelon 6, 13
Argentinosaurus 6
Australian animals 22–23

B

Bengal tigers 30

C

Carolina parakeets 7
cave bears 15
climate 4, 5, 11, 15
cockroaches 24
cod 27
coelacanths 25
Cretaceous period 10, 12, 22
crocodiles 10, 12, 24

D

Deinosuchus 12
Devonian period 6
dinosaurs 4, 5, 6, 8, 10-11, 12, 24
diprotodon 22
dodos 7, 16–17
Dunkleosteus 6

E

ekaltadeta 22
elephant birds 18
endangered animals 30
extinction 4–5, 22, 26, 28

F

fossils 8–9, 25

G

giant echidnas 22
golden lion tamarins 30
gorillas 29

H

Haast's eagles 18, 19

I

Ice Age 4, 14–15
insects 10, 24, 26, 29
Irish elk 14

K

kangaroos 22, 23

L

lions 15, 22
Liopleurodon 12, 13

M

Macrauchenias 7
mammals 10, 12, 22, 29
marsupials 22
mass extinctions 5, 8, 10, 26
megalania 22
meteor 5, 11
moas 7, 18, 19
mosasaurs 6, 12, 13

N

Nile crocodiles 25

O

orangutans 29
overharvesting 4, 27

P

Platecarpus 12
Platybelodon 7
plesiosaurs 12, 13
pollution 26
procoptodon 22
Pteranodon 6, 13
pterosaurs 5, 12, 13

Q

quaggas 7, 20–21
Quetzalcoatlus 13
quinkana 22

R

radiocarbon dating 15
reptiles 8, 12–13, 22, 24, 29

S

sharks 24, 25
Smilodon 7
Steller's sea cow 7

T

Tasmanian tiger 6, 7, 23
thylacine *see* Tasmanian tiger
tuna 27
Tylosaurus 13

W

wildlife organizations 29, 30
woolly mammoths 4, 14, 15
woolly rhinoceroses 7, 14, 15

Z

zebras 20
zoologists 29